MAKING CONTACT DURING EMERGENCIES

Mark and Krista Lawley

Published by Mark and Krista Lawley

Distributed by Kindle Direct Publishing

Introduction

There have been many books written on the topic of "emergency communications," EMCOMM, or ECOMM,: personal communications plans, communications for preppers, long-term back-up power solutions and the building of radio systems for use during disasters and SHTF ("stuff" hits the fan – well, we are keeping it clean for families, but you can translate).rinting

This book is different; it's about getting help when you need it. Hikers, hunters, boaters, outdoor enthusiasts, or anyone who wants to be prepared to communicate, or get help in an emergency, will benefit from this information.

o   This book is designed to give you information, which, if acted upon, might save your life, the life of a loved one, or someone you may come across who is in need of help.

o   This book will help the novice learn methods of communicating, attracting attention, and making your presence known.

o   It will help those who are prepared to think through communicating, getting help, and bringing new ideas to light.

Our research for this book revealed a deficiency in our own ECOMM preparations which was quickly remedied, adding another tool in the toolbox which may assist us in getting help when we need it.

"Making Contact During Emergencies" came out of an effort to produce an emergency communications plan for our extended family members in North Carolina, Georgia, Virginia, Colorado, Tennessee, and several cities in Alabama. We developed a list of names, phone numbers, and e-mail addresses to distribute to each family member for use before, during, and after natural disasters affecting any of us directly such as, but not limited to, hurricanes, wildfires, or winter storms.

The idea was that, once any family member outside the effected area was contacted by family inside the effected area, and reports received, information would then be relayed to all other family members via normal communication methods, i.e.

group texts, cell phones, and Facebook group posts being the quickest.

Due to our having several licensed amateur radio operators in the family, we added call signs, local repeaters, Echolink node codes, and designated frequencies to the list.

Eventually, instructions were added which included how to communicate over long distances with small, inexpensive handheld radios capable of making these contacts and having those frequencies preprogrammed. Some of the non-licensed family members have also purchased radios "just in case," and two are currently working toward obtaining amateur radio licenses (it's really not hard at all).

As our family emergency communications plan grew, we realized that there were others concerned about being able to communicate immediately after a disaster, and others who may need to communicate with someone, or anyone, in order to get help on the way after an accident, whether for themselves, a companion, or someone found in distress along the way.

In this book, we will illustrate the need for emergency communications and assume you have already decided there is a need to "be prepared".

We will feature equipment ranging from your cell phone to a full-blown amateur radio (HAM radio) station; and will introduce the possibility of using unconventional (and possibly controversial) frequencies in the event of an actual emergency, such as "someone needs help NOW, or that someone will likely die".

Modern equipment allows us to communicate without spending a small fortune; actually, it can be quite inexpensive, especially when compared to the value your life, that of a loved one, or perhaps someone you encounter, whether it be a hiker on the Appalachian Trail, a motor vehicle accident victim, or the neighbor down the street having chest pain while cutting grass.

The best definition we've seen of a "prepper" is someone preparing to be a survivor if the need ever arises.

This book is not about bullets, beans, and band-aids, it's not about bug-out locations, storing food and water, or developing alternative energy sources in case the grid goes down. It's not really about being able to communicate across the state or nation after the SHTF, though it could help. It's about YOU being prepared to communicate during and after an emergency. It's about getting help when it's needed. It's not limited to "preppers" but is intended for hikers, campers, hunters, anglers, boaters and anyone who goes into the great outdoors or anywhere normal communications may not be available.

It will also be a reference resource for unconventional frequencies which might be used *ONLY* in true life-or-death situations to save your life or someone else's, and will guide you on how to make a call on those frequencies.

MODES AND METHODS OF COMMUNICATIONS

When you need help during an emergency, or when you are awaiting word from a loved one inside the impact area of a natural disaster, *how* you communicate doesn't matter; *that* you communicate does.

The old pen, paper, envelope and stamp method is too slow. Landlines may be down. Video calling requires a cellular or internet connection which may not be available, especially in remote areas or impact areas after a disaster. These are some of the methods and modes of communications which work when other modes fail.

CELL PHONES

The first thing to do is try the most widely used form of communication available today: the telephone. Dial 911 in an emergency. Call family and friends after a disaster. If it works, you've communicated; problem solved.

Note: Federal law requires that all cell phones be able to dial 911 if they can be powered up, regardless of whether or not they are connected to a carrier. I've often recommended that people without a cell phone obtain an unused phone, keep it charged, and carry it with them, on their person, in case of emergency, and keep it by the bedside at night. It will dial 911 only, so be sure that it's truly an emergency or serious matter. This is especially useful for shut-ins who use a landline phone, in case the landline goes out. It is also advisable that those living alone, who do not have some type of "Life Alert" system, carry the phone on them in case of a fall. Without having to try to get to the landline, they can simply pull out the "911-only" cell phone and call for help.

This exact situation occurred with a family member recently. She fell, broke bones and was unable to get up. Having her cell phone on her person allowed her to summon help from a family member a few blocks away, and she called 911 to get medical help on the way.

Sometimes, cell phone traffic becomes overloaded or inoperable, as is often the case after a tornado. If that happens, try text messaging. Text messages use much less bandwidth than voice or video calls, and you may find that you are able to communicate via text when it is nearly impossible to complete a voice call.

This was certainly the case for our family during the April 27, 2011 tornadoes which passed through Alabama, taking 353 lives. We were in a shelter in Riverside, Alabama, manning the HAM radio and watching every source of weather information available to us, including GRLevel 3® radar from Gibson Ridge® – weather nerds really need to check this one out; there's a fully operational free trial. www.grlevelx.com

We watched as one of the tornadoes tracked across an area about 40 miles away, an area where two of our daughters and their families lived at the time.

It was 20 minutes before they were able to get a text message to us letting us know they were safe. It took another two hours before a voice call was completed.

On that night, one son-in-law decided he would obtain his amateur radio license so we would be able to communicate almost instantly, if ever again put in that situation. Twenty minutes is a LONG time to wait to hear your family is safe.

SATELLITE COMMUNICATIONS

There are numerous satellite devices and systems available to the public today, but we will limit this portion to three in particular, which allow communications from any point on the earth.

Satellite Phones

There are numerous satellite communications companies providing voice and data communications from anywhere on the earth. Depending on the service package, prices range from around $5.00 per minute to $16.00 per minute, at the time of this writing. The equipment is expensive, at a thousand dollars or more, per unit, and subscriptions are required. They have their place and purpose, and serve the needs of many around the world, but there are better, more cost effective satellite communications options for the average person who travels outside the areas well covered by cellular services, such as backcountry hikers, private pilots, and off-shore vessels. Let's explore.

InReach Satellite Tracker®

The InReach Satellite Tracker offered by Garmin® and DeLorme® is to satellite communications what "Help, I've fallen and can't get up" is to home-use landline alert systems.

The units themselves are relatively small, easily carried in a back pack or pilot's map case, worn on a belt, or carried in a glove box, and prices for the units begin under $300.00.

The units provide an emergency activation button which sends a signal to a monitoring center complete with GPS coordinates. The units are text enabled, which can be sent to any cell phone or texting device. In the case of an emergency activation, the monitoring center will establish text communications confirming the emergency, the location, and the extent of the need. The units can be used to text with rescuers to coordinate the resources necessary to attend to those in need.

At the time of this writing, packages run around $12 per month on an annual contract, or $15 per month for occasional users, as the package can be suspended and reactivated when needed. A web search will provide more than enough information to allow the reader to make an informed decision.

Personal Locator Beacons

A personal locator beacon (PLB) is a satellite device providing one-way communication. Similar to aviation emergency location transmitters (ELT) carried on aircraft, and Marine EPIRBs, the units send a digital signal to the SARSAT Search and Rescue Satellite system when activated.

The units are priced as low as $ 250 for very basic PLBs, which send a basic radio signal to more expensive units which incorporate GPS and are able to transmit your actual location with the distress message.

Another type of PLB is the marine Emergency Position Indicating Radio Beacon (EPIRB), which is used in case of an emergency out at sea. Maritime law requires at least one EPIRB on each ship, and is used to locate ships, lifeboats, life rafts, or people adrift at sea.

EPIRBs may be activated manually, with some models being capable of activating automatically when it makes contact with water.

(for more info see www.marineinsight.com)

Avalanche Beacons

Avalanche beacons are a vital piece of safety equipment if you spend time skiing, snowshoeing, or snowboarding in the backcountry. These units emit a pulsed radio signal in case you are buried in an avalanche.

Here's how it works; rather than sending out a general signal over long distances, this PLB sends a low power signal to other members of your party, or those nearby, equipped with similar devices which are able to receive a signal transmitted by your beacon facilitating the search. Prices start around $350.00, but are vital for those skiing in the backcountry. See www.rei.com for more information on avalanche beacons.

PLBs do not require a subscription, (but do require registration), and are to be used ONLY in an emergency, as once an activation signal is received, contact with you or your contact list is attempted to establish if it is a false alarm. If they're unable to confirm a false alarm, then search and rescue teams will be dispatched.

If you fly, or spend a lot of time in the backcountry, buy a PLB with GPS capability. Your life is surely worth more than the additional investment.

Search "personal locator beacons" for more detailed information.

RADIO COMMUNICATIONS

A little understanding is necessary when considering radio use for emergency communications, but we'll keep it simple for the purposes of this book. There are many good resources if you would like to develop an in-depth working knowledge of radio theory, operations, and the opportunities for involvement in amateur radio operations. For example, www.arrl.org is a great place to start for learning the basics of amateur radio.

The radio operations we will feature in this book are divided into three basic categories, or bands: HF (High Frequency), VHF (Very High Frequency), and UHF (Ultra High Frequency). Radio frequencies referenced in this book are measured in megahertz (MHz)

The actual frequencies are:

- o   HF: 3 MHz - 30 MHz or 100 meters - 10 meters

- o   VHF: 30 MHz - 300 MHz or 10 meters - 1 meter

- o   UHF: 300Hz – 3 GHz (gigahertz)

HF is used for shortwave radio, some aviation communications, government time stations, amateur radio, and citizens band communications, among others. Radio waves in this band can be bounced back to earth by the ionosphere, allowing very long range, even worldwide communications.

VHF is used for more local communications, the distance of which can be increased by height, antenna gain, and directional antennas. VHF is often used by FM radio broadcasting, television, and marine and land mobile radio stations i.e., some public service, police departments, fire departments, and emergency medical services, amateur radio, FRS and GMRS services, as well as aircraft ground and airborne operations. VHF is primarily "line of sight" communications, but does work reasonably well in mountainous areas.

UHF is used for television broadcasting, GPS, personal radio services, some cordless phones, Wi-Fi, Bluetooth, walkie-talkies and many other applications. UHF is primarily "line of sight" communications. It is often blocked by hills, mountains, and large buildings. It does seem to work well through interior walls, making it great for indoor operation.

One-Way Radio Communications

o   One-way radio communications are either:

o   Transmit-only, as are most personal locator beacons, as well as broadcast radio or television stations, and are designed to send information or data out.

o   Receive-only radios, as in AM/FM radios, weather radios, and scanners. These are used for entertainment or to receive

information or data, and they have no
capability to transmit.

Two Way Radio Communications

Two-way radio systems usually operate in a
half-duplex mode. Unlike full duplex systems such
as telephones, where both parties can talk and hear
simultaneously, half-duplex systems are either/or.
You can either transmit or receive. One party presses
the transmit button while the other listens, then the
roles are reversed.

All of the radios we will feature in this book
operate in the half-duplex mode.

Simplex Operation

Simplex operation utilizes one frequency to
both transmit and receive. It is used radio to radio,
and is limited in the distance over which the radios
may communicate.

Simplex operation may be utilized anywhere
two radios are set to the same frequency and the
radios are within range, and that range may be
decreased depending on terrain, buildings, or large
obstacles.

I have used radios on simplex frequencies
while hunting, fishing, and even with family spread
out in the mall or at an event, both on the amateur
radio bands as well as the Family Radio Services,
depending on whether or not the other radio operator
held a current amateur radio license.

I have also used simplex frequencies in both the police and fire bands where shorter distance communications were needed, such as search and rescue, or on-scene operations.

Repeater Operation

In repeater operations the radios utilize two frequencies and a repeater. The simple explanation is that the radios transmit on the frequency that the repeater receives, and the repeater simultaneously retransmits on the frequency that is received by the radios.

Repeater antennas are usually placed on top of towers located on mountains and tall buildings. This height, and the higher power levels utilized by the repeater, enables communication over much longer distances, especially with mobile and handheld radios. Repeaters are used extensively in amateur radio, commercial/business, and public service systems.

Repeater frequencies must be pre-programmed into your radio, along with any required privacy tones (PL Tones) before the repeater may be used. Repeater programming can be done from the keypad or microphone on most hand held and mobile radios, but most of us find it much easier to program from the computer. We'll provide this information in more detail later, when we discuss CHIRP programming software.

Radio Services

Let's talk about some of the radio services available which may be used in emergency communication. Remember, "emergency communication" usually means you are away from home, on the trail, in the woods or on the water, or traveling, so most of the discussion will involve portable radios.

Family Radio Service

The Family Radio Service (FRS) is a two-way, short-distance communications service authorized by the FCC in 1996. It's designed to accommodate family and group short range communication needs using small handheld radios.

The FRS utilizes 22 channelized frequencies in the 462 MHz and 467 MHz range. An individual license is not required, there's no minimum age requirement, and it may be used for personal or business reasons, as long as you comply with the rules.

FRS channels 1-7 and 15-22 may utilize up to two watts of power, and channels 8-14 are limited to one-half watt. Later, we will provide a list of channels advertised on some forums where different groups can be found after the SHTF.

General Mobile Radio Service

The GMRS is comprised of thirty channelized frequencies in the 462 MHz and 467 MHz range (UHF). Yes, it's the same frequency range as the FRS, but they are interspersed between the FRS frequencies. The FCC allows repeater use on some of the GMRS channels as well as limited data applications, such as text messaging across the system.

The General Mobile Radio Service (GMRS) requires an FCC license (good for ten years) according to Rule Part 47 C.F.R. part 95 subpart E. You may apply for a license if you are 18 years of age or older, but any family member regardless of age, may operate the radio under that license.

The radios often purchased at sporting goods and big-box stores, and labeled as "26 mile radios", are usually in the FRS and/or GMRS bands. Don't count on that "26 miles" unless you happen to be at sea, climb the sailing mast, and make contact with someone else at the top of their mast 26 miles away. They are good, though, for that which they are designed: short-range family or group communications, and they certainly have a place in communications after a disaster or SHTF situation.

Imagine if your entire neighborhood had these radios, all set to the same channel, and ready to use during and after disasters. Trapped survivors might be located and rescued sooner, the injured located and attended more rapidly, or the rest of the neighborhood informed of hazards in a more timely fashion.

Multi-Use Radio Service

The Multi-Use Radio Service (MURS) is comprised of five channelized frequencies in the 151-154 MHz range (VHF). MURS transmissions are limited to a maximum of two watts of power output. Range of these radios is limited to a short-range distance of about two miles, but an external antenna can extend that range out to as much as ten miles. I have used the MURS while traveling in a group, and with the use of magnetic VHF antennas, I have experienced solid communications out to seven miles on the road.

The MURS does not require an individual license, and there is no age restriction on operating on the MURS band.

Amateur Radio

Amateur Radio just may be the absolute best radio communications system for emergency communications available during and after any disaster or SHTF situation. Local disaster organization such as ARES (Amateur Radio Emergency Services) as well as individual operators WILL be on-the-air during and after local severe weather situations, tornadoes, hurricanes, or man-made disasters. Many will deploy to provide coordinated communications from shelters, Emergency Management Operations Centers, (EMA EOC), Red Cross and Salvation Army centers, command posts, and sometimes in search and rescue (SAR) operations.

Amateur radio (HAM radio) operators have been instrumental in helping to locate missing children, dementia patients, elderly people, as well as providing essential communications into and out of severely damaged disaster areas where all other communications have been lost. When all else fails, HAM radio WORKS!

Amateur Radio encompasses many modes of communication ranging from old-school Morse Code, (referred to as CW or continuous wave), to satellite communications, voice communications, telegraphy, even television transmissions via HAM radio across twenty-seven frequency bands.

Some bands are used for local communication through simplex (single frequency), or by using repeaters. Mobile radios operate with as much as 80 watts, base stations with amplifiers up to 1500 watts on some bands, and handheld radios operating at 8 watts are now available. Other bands can accommodate world-wide and inter-continental communications on HF.

Eighty meters is a band where regular communications across several states can be found. One night, in the central Alabama woods, in a camper with my son-in-law, using a mobile radio (Yaesu 857D) powered off a car battery under the table, and a very temporary 14 gauge wire strung across two trees, I participated in a "rag chew" with folks in Florida, North Carolina, Mississippi, and Texas, with a few others around the country popping in at times.

A license is required, and there are currently three licenses available, and each requires a test.

Morse Code is no longer required for any license class, but it is still alive and well on HAM radio, and can establish contact when other means fail.

The Technician Class license is the first level license available. The Technician test isn't very hard, if you study a bit, and study guides and practice tests are available online for all classes.

HAMTESTONLINE.COM® is an online resource which, for a fee, provides study material on each subject, provides explanations and helpful hints to remember correct answers, and provides practice tests. At the time of this writing, the listed price for the technician class study course is $24.95 which includes a 100% money back guarantee.

Study guide books may be purchased for each license class, and the question pool from which test questions are selected may be downloaded in printable form from the American Radio Relay League (ARRL) website at www.arrl.org at no cost.

If you elect to go with purchasing study guides, QRZ.com® is a site that provides practice tests at no cost, and has helped many amateur radio operators pass the tests.

Technician class operators are licensed to operate on all frequencies in the amateur bands 50 MHz and above, and have limited privileges in the ten-meter band (28.300 – 28.500), which at times allows world-wide contacts to be made.

This license class covers the two-meter (144.00 - 148.00 VHF) and the seventy-centimeter (420.00 – 450.00 UHF) bands, where most local and repeater communications take place. The majority of new Technicians begin on the two-meter band, make local contacts, make new friends, and even get involved in any number of activities involving HAM radio. Activities include amateur radio clubs, ARES (Amateur Radio Emergency Services), SKYWARN (weather spotting), public service events, providing communications for marathons, bike rides, and even endurance horse rides through national forests where cell phones are not reliable. Many search-and-rescue (SAR) teams and disaster relief teams are composed of HAM radio volunteers, or have at least one (referred to as a 'communicator') on the team.

Here's a good illustration for you. On the weekend of the writing of this particular section of the book, a group of HAM radio friends are camping in the east Alabama woods of the Talladega National Forest providing communications for the Yellowhammer Endurance Horse Ride.

Twelve checkpoints throughout the trail route and a base station located at the ride command center (fancy term for under a tent in the stable area) are manned by HAM radio operators and unlicensed volunteers, as riders compete in a three day event involving 75-mile, 50-mile, and 25-mile events. (I can't imagine riding 75 miles in a day on a HORSE, but these folks do it in an area where cell phones are useful ONLY if you drive to the top of the nearest mountain, stand on the back of the truck with one arm and one leg raised, and then you might get a cell signal, if you don't fall off the truck).

I can tell you this for sure, these operators are protecting lives! Even with the long hours, cold winds, and sleeping in a tent or camper, these operators are having the time of their lives and wouldn't be anywhere else this weekend, if at all possible. I only wish my wife and I could be there with them this year.

I have participated in most of the above activities across my years as a licensed amateur radio operator, and have seen the presence of a HAM radio operator lead to the saving of a life in getting timely emergency medical assistance, even in the middle of nowhere. Both licensed and unlicensed volunteers are welcome at most of these events, and your assistance will be greatly appreciated, and you will find many of these events to be personally rewarding.

General and Extra Class licenses open up a lot more band space in which to operate, especially in the HF bands. General and Extra class license holders may operate in the lower bands, even down to 3.4 MHz (80 meters) and 1.8 MHz (160 meters) which, at times, provide world-wide communications, including Antarctica.

The difference in General and Extra Classes on an operational level is that Extra class has a little more operating space across some bands. Both classes can do the exact same thing, with the Extra Class Operator being able to do it in a little more band space.

I would recommend anyone interested in communicating after a large impact area, communications-interrupting disaster, SHTF situation, or anyone just wanting to talk across the nation or internationally, study and obtain at least a General Class license.

CB Radio

The Citizen Band Radio Service, or CB for short, was created by the FCC in 1945. It is a form of radio intended to be used for short range communications, can be used for personal or business use, and no longer requires a license.

Though CB radio should not be considered a viable replacement for amateur (Ham) radio, the radios do have their place, and should be a part of the communications preps for survivalists and preppers.

Even though CB radio reached its peak of popularity in the 1970s, there are many people who still use CB as a hobby. It is also used by members of hunting and fishing clubs, and cross-country travelers.

Most truck drivers use CB radios to share updates on weather conditions, traffic conditions, detours, and even the locations of police running radar.

Depending on the antenna, mobile and handheld CB radios are usually limited to four or five miles under normal conditions, at the legal power limit of four watts.

The CB radio frequency spectrum is divided into forty channels and may be used in AM mode and USB (upper side band) mode. The most commonly monitored channels are the emergency channel 9

(27.065 MHz) and the channel most used by truckers and travelers is channel 19 (27.185 MHz).

If your activities are limited to areas within about five miles of the interstate system, a CB radio may be a viable means of communicating during an emergency situation, though it might require that you get to the top of a hill to contact passing motorists. CB radios can be useful in disaster impact areas as normal cell service is often interrupted when cell towers are damaged or overloaded. CB radios would be excellent in communicating with neighbors within a small community or sub-division, and could be used not only during emergency situations, but for community events.

For survivalists and preppers, CB radio is just another tool in the toolbox, to be utilized in their communications plan.

VHF Marine Radio, or VHF Maritime Mobile Radio

Most VHF Marine radios on the market today have in excess of twenty-five usable channels, and are available as rechargeable handheld radios, mobile radios mounted in boats (and sometimes vehicles), and base radios used on-shore, inside buildings, with antennas mounted outside and elevated for greater distance.

In general, VHF marine radios have a radio-to-radio range of about 5-10 miles, and at least 20 miles to a US Coast Guard station.

The FCC requires that any boat equipped with a VHF marine radio keep a watch on channel 16 (156.800 MHz) whenever the radio isn't being used to communicate. Channel 16 is recognized worldwide as the distress, safety and calling channel, and is used by the US Coast Guard to make urgent broadcasts and weather warnings. Channel 16 is constantly monitored by the USCG, and has the best chance of being received by someone in an emergency.

Marine radio frequencies could be a viable option for emergency communications if you are within a few miles of one of America's navigable waterways. Most "open" VHF radios are capable of being programmed to operate on 156.800 MHz, and that frequency is programmed into my handheld radios, as I live just a few miles off the Tennessee River.

Note: I can hear someone screaming, "You can't do that" when they read the next two radio services, but let's remember that according to the FCC rules, anyone can talk on any frequency during a TRUE emergency (someone's life is at stake), so I will include both services and how they can be accessed during a true emergency.

AirBand or Aircraft Band or Aeronautical Band Radios

The aircraft band is a set of VHF frequencies used for AM voice transmissions. These frequencies are used for both ground operations at airports and communications to and from aircraft while in flight.

Airband voice transmissions can be completed from as much as 200 miles on a good weather day from an aircraft flying at 35,000 feet.

Handheld airband radios for civilian aviation can be purchased for a little under two hundred dollars, and can go up to whatever you want to invest. The higher-end handhelds have navigational programming as well as GPS. For our purposes here, the lower cost radios will do just fine in the case of a true emergency. It's just a matter of waiting until you see an aircraft overhead. I've not seen radios available which will transmit on the military frequencies, but I'm sure they can be found.

Civilian aircraft operate between 118.00 MHz and 136.975 MHz, and the monitored emergency, or "Guard frequency" is 121.5 MHz.

Military aircraft operate VHF AM between 225.0 MHz and 399.95 MHz. The monitored or "Guard frequency" is 243.0 MHz.

Again, these frequencies require authorization to transmit, but, in the case of a true life-threatening emergency situation, we can argue that point once everyone is safe.

Police/Fire/Public Service/Utility Radio

First, it is NEVER a good idea to talk on any radio service frequency for which you are not licensed or authorized. All agency 'licensed' frequencies such as police, fire, ambulance, and even Red Cross frequencies require permission to use. There are MOUs (memorandum of understanding, or agreements) between groups such as Southern Baptist Disaster Relief and the Red Cross. Southern Baptists prepare 80% of the food distributed by the Red Cross in disasters, so communication is necessary between the two groups. Police departments do a similar thing in allowing other, nearby agencies to use each other's frequencies in time of need.

So, I'll say it again: It is never a good idea (or legal) to talk on public service, military, or aircraft frequencies, UNLESS a life is on the line, in a TRUE EMERGENCY.

With that said public service frequencies are available at www.radioreference.com and are broken down by state, county, and city. Most frequencies for which a government entity is licensed are listed.

Most of these frequencies are linked to a repeater which requires a "PL Tone" to access, and those tones or codes are not listed. This does not, however, make the frequency inoperable in times of emergency communications. It means that the repeater will not be available to us, and that we will have to use the simplex frequency, which will limit the range of the transmissions, but can still be used. In fact, the very same setup is programmed into most police radios as a "talk-around" frequency for use in times of repeater failure or in short distance situations.

If I am going to travel to an out-of-town location, I will often look up the frequencies for the local police departments and fire departments and program them into my handheld radio. I've never used them, but I feel like it is better to have them "just in case.

"Talking" On A Radio During Emergencies

In the event you do have to use your radio for emergency communications, it is best to use "plain language" while communicating. That means NO "10 codes," "Q-signals" or "good-buddy" language. Be clear, concise, and to the point – USE PLAIN LANGUAGE, and use clean language.

There are no standardized set of codes or signals across the various agencies or radio services. Most fire departments and many police departments have gone to plain language in their radio communications, and all do when called upon during times of interoperability. An example of differing ten-codes is that a 10-97 at my former department was a "fight" and at my current department 10-97 means we "have arrived on the scene." You can imagine the confusion if departments didn't use plain language when communicating with each other. You might call for an ambulance and a wrecker shows up.

Radio Communications Equipment

Handheld Radios

Let's consider portable handheld radio equipment when preparing for emergency communications.

There are many great brands of handheld radios available, variously referred to as HTs (handi-talkies) or WTs (walkie talkies). A search will reveal more than you may care to browse through, and at every price level you can imagine.

Handheld radios may be single-band or multi-band, meaning that they will transmit on VHF or UHF (single-band), or VHF and UHF (multi-band), and single-band HF in the case of CB radios. Most business-band handhelds, and FRS or GMRS radios, will be single band. Amateur handhelds are available in either single or multi bands. The "tri-band" amateur handheld radios are still VHF and UHF, but will operate in the two-meter (144 MHz), twenty-three centimeter (220 MHz), and the seventy-centimeter (440 MHz) bands.

These handheld radios are hard programmed to operate within specific frequency ranges for their intended purpose. Some may receive outside that band, such as broadcast radio or weather radio frequencies, but will transmit only within the intended frequency range.

We recognize that there are handheld radios available on many other bands, but those are not being featured here. One class of radio we will discuss here is the multi-band, VHF/UHF radios which are "open" and may be programmed across the entire VHF/UHF bands. These radios are controversial in some circles, and adored in others.

We own several of these radios, and have found them very useful on a personal level. Being in law enforcement, I have the law enforcement agency and fire department frequencies for my county programmed into the radio. Being a HAM radio operator, I have the local repeaters programmed in, as well as those in several surrounding counties. As a grandfather, I have FRS/GMRS programmed for traveling with family or for when the youngsters come over and play "Army" or "FBI" behind the house. (Yes, I've been the "bad-guy" several times and usually get shot with a Nerf gun).

In the 'prepper' community, and among many survivalists, these are very popular radios, and I recommend them as well for anyone who spends much time hiking, hunting, fishing, camping, off-roading, or just relaxing in the back country. They are presented here in no particular order:

Tytera® (TYT) MD-2017 $159.00

Power: 5 watts output
Modes: digital and analog
Fqs: UHF: 400-480 / VHF: 136-174
Simplex and Repeater programmable
PC programming recommended
Features:
IP67 waterproof
GPS Module

Single call, Group call, All call selectable
Remote Stun/Kill/Activate capable

The remote stun/kill/activate feature is appreciated in the prepper community as the radio may be disabled remotely by a partner's radio in the event a radio is seized by someone you would not wish to have the ability to know your operational frequencies or receive your transmissions. Yes, any other radio could be used to receive, IF they are able to find you, or figure out your operational security, and at best may only be able to receive one side of the transmissions if you are using separate frequencies for transmit and receive, but this feature takes care of it, if that is a concern of yours.

Lone Worker Mode:

The "lone worker" feature allows the user to set a defined time limit in which the user must "check in" by pressing the transmit button. If that time expires without the "check-in" it sounds a reminder tone and if the transmit button is not pressed within a set time, the radio sends out an emergency signal.

Emergency Alert:

The radio sends out an emergency alert to other radios, in several preconfigured modes, and can be operated manually or through the "Lone Worker mode".

Tytera® (TYT) MD-380 $99

Power: 5/1 watts selectable output
Modes: digital and analog
Fqs: UHF: 400-480 / VHF: 136-174
Simplex and Repeater programmable
PC programming required
Features: This radio has basically the same
features as the newest model, the MD-2017,
but it is not waterproof, and the GPS module
is an add-on option.

Baofeng® UV-5R $25-$30

Modes: Analog only
Power: 4/1 Watts selectable output
Fqs: UHF: 400-520 / VHF: 136-174
/Simplex and Repeater programmable
PC programming recommended

Baofeng® BF-F8HP $62

Mode: Analog only
Power: 8/4/1 Watts selectable output
Fqs: UHF: 400-520 / VHF: 136-174
Simplex and Repeater programmable
PC programming recommended

Wouxun® KG-UV6X $15

Mode: Analog only
Power: 5/1 Watts selectable output
Fqs: UHF: 406-512 / VHF: 136-174
Simplex and Repeater programmable
Meets IP55 waterproofing rating
PC programming recommended

Wouxun® KG-UV3X Pro $139

Mode: Analog only
Power: 5/1 Watts selectable output
Fqs: UHF: 406-512 / VHF: 136-174
Simplex and Repeater programmable
Meets IP55 waterproofing rating
PC programming recommended

Do you remember that anyone may transmit on any frequency during an actual emergency? Let me relate a real-life emergency where a donated 4-watt handheld radio saved a life.

Long's Electronics in Birmingham, Alabama, was a long-time retailer of HAM radio equipment. After discontinuing their line of radios, they had a half-dozen Midland handheld radios sitting on a shelf in the back room. They decided to donate them to our disaster relief organization, and I picked up the radios. I was charging the batteries, programming frequencies, and testing the radios in the camper at the hunting club (in the middle of nowhere).

A friend and fellow disaster relief volunteer took me up on an invitation to go deer hunting. On a frosty-cold morning, with temps not expected to rise out of the twenties, we met and went to the camper to make final preparations for a day in the backwoods.

Before leaving the camper, I handed him one of the radios, showed him where to turn it on and demonstrated "press to talk, release to listen" and told him to call me if he needed me.

I dropped him off in an area where I regularly saw deer, and told him I would pick him up a little after dark, then took off to another area about five-hundred yards away. He put his new tree stand together and went up a tree overlooking a place surely to be passed through by that monster buck we all dreamed of bagging.

An hour of so later I hear his voice on my handheld radio saying, "Mark, you're going to have to come help me, I've fallen out of the tree." A weld on his brand new tree stand had broken causing him to fall out backwards from a height of about twelve feet.

To make a long story short, he had broken his back. I was not planning to pick him up for another nine hours or so, and the temp was about 24 degrees. Through the use of a small handheld radio, he was able to call for help, and through a team effort we were able to get him out of the woods and to the hospital. He told me later that his doctor had told him that he may not have lived with the injury and extreme cold (for the south, anyway) had he not been able to get help when he did. A real-life success story for emergency communications being available when needed!

Mobile Radios

The handheld radio is the lightest, most portable radio you can have, and it is highly recommended that you have at least one, if not several, in your arsenal of communication tools.

However, there are times when you may need more than a handheld radio to establish communications; hence, the mobile radio.

Mobile radios operate on 12 volts, and may be mounted in a vehicle, operated in any area with a 12 volt battery, or utilizing a 12-volt power supply.

Mobile radios are available which operate on as little as 0.5 watts, or as much as 100 watts. There are single-band radios and some are multi-band radios. Some mobile radios cover HF, VHF, and UHF. Many HAM operators utilize a mobile radio and power supply as their primary "base" radio.

I personally have a Yaesu® 857D multi-band radio and a 35-amp 12-volt power supply set up in my office/radio room. This combination has served me well for over a decade. I've taken it into the woods and operated on a 12-volt car battery, as well as carrying it half way across the country and operating it with a 12-volt "jump box" designed for jumping a car with a dead battery.   I've used this radio from the office, truck, and in the woods to make hundreds of contacts around the world.

The mobile is worthy of consideration if you take your vehicle into areas off the beaten path, camping, hunting, fishing, four-wheeling, or anywhere else where you may not have reliable cell service.

Antennas

A friend once told me that a thousand dollar radio and a ten dollar antenna is a ten dollar system, and that a one-hundred dollar radio with a hundred-dollar antenna will out talk it any day. I have found that to be pretty much a universal truth across the board. Do not cut corners on your antenna. You WILL regret it.

There are as many antenna options as there are radios available. The worth of many is questionable, especially when used across any kind of distance. We'll limit this section to those which may be used as portable, mobile, or in the back country. Let's consider a few:

The "Rubber-Duck" antenna, which comes with most handheld radios, is a fantastic little antenna when used in the back yard as the grandsons play "Army" or when you need to communicate over a limited distance. In my experience, the "rubber-duck" is good for a few miles when using a repeater, and maybe a mile or so on simplex.

The "magnetic-mount" antenna is actually a very versatile option, depending on the actual antenna used. Some are available using rare-earth magnets with a short whip (12"-18") and are very usable on VHF and UHF. Other mounts are available which will accept any antenna designed for that mount. I have a Larsen VHF/UHF antenna on a magnetic mount on my Jeep at this time. It was permanently mounted on my last pickup truck, and will be again soon on the Patriot, but for the moment it is a magnetic-mount.

The magnetic mount also works well when traveling in another person's vehicle, with either a mobile on a lighter plug (must use low power to prevent blowing the lighter plug fuses), or a handie-talkie with a connector adaptor between the radio and antenna. Some of these with shorter whips and about 12 feet of coax will fit into a backpack or bag.

The "Roll-Up J-Pole" is an antenna made from approximately 60 inches of flat TV twin-lead and a short run of coax. This is an easy DIY project, or it may be purchased commercially. As the name implies, it easily rolls up to fit into a backpack or bag. When needed, the antenna is unrolled, pulled up into a tree with string or rope, placed on a pole, or tacked to a wall and connected to the handheld or mobile radio.

The antenna we use on our handheld radios is the Nagoya® NA-771 15.6" whip antenna. These antennas WORK! I have been able to use repeaters 5-

6 miles away from inside the house, and 15 or more miles away when standing outside.

Noting the test results that were reported by substituting the antenna which came with the handheld radio with a Nagoya® 701 antenna, this seems like a 'must do' item for everyone and all situations. The Nagoya® 701 antenna is about the same weight, and 3″ longer (7¾″) but still more than sufficiently portable for almost all situations.

Be careful, though, as there are some knock-offs out there for under $10 which will not give the same performance as the "Authentic Genuine Nagoya® NA-771". Expect to pay around $17-$20 at the time of this writing, in 2019, and be sure to order the right connection for your selected radios. You wont regret the investment.

PROGRAMMING RADIOS

Regardless which radio you choose, BUY THE PROGRAMMING CABLE, if it is not provided with the radio! Many of the handheld radios available today are not the easiest thing to program from the front panel, and some are darn near impossible. Did I mention that you WILL want the programming cable?

Most all have software available, either with the radio or downloadable, which will make the programming easier. Some are intuitive and others may make you pull out your own hair.

The good news is that there is a great solution available. Keep reading.

CHIRP Radio Software® is available free from chirpsoftware.com. CHIRP is a free, open source tool for programming your radio. The software is easy to use for programming simplex or repeater frequencies, including the tones necessary to operate through repeaters. They may be entered individually, or copied from other sources and pasted into a file for your radio. It easily allows cloning from one radio to another, or programming a set or group of radios with the same set of frequencies.

The software has a number of stock configurations available from the pull-down menus, including FRS/GMRS channels, MURS channels, marine VHF channels, and even railroad channels. These can be copied and pasted into a file and other frequencies entered to create your personal radio configuration file. Changes are easy to make, and adding a frequency at any time is as simple as opening your CHIRP file, adding the frequency, and writing, or uploading, it to the radio.

You can also import frequencies from well-known websites such as www.repeaterbook.com® and www.radioreference.com®.

www.repeaterbook.com provides amateur radio repeater frequencies across the nation, arranged by location, and the RepeaterBook® app gives you amateur radio repeaters within a set distance from your location, and all the information necessary for using that repeater.

www.Radioreference.com® is a scanner frequency and radio communications reference database. Arranged by states, counties, agencies, and services, Radioreference.com® provides a wealth of information for listening to various agencies. This is a vital tool when you need to locate frequencies which might be a lifesaver in a true emergency.

Another great use for these "open" radios is as a scanner for public service agencies such as fire, police, and EMS. A friend has her Baofeng® UV-5R programmed to receive all of her surrounding law enforcement and fire departments, as well as two local HAM repeaters which are active during weather situations. She is not licensed under any radio service, but listens to get great information. Where else can you buy a great little portable scanner for $25?

Programming Simplex

Programming simplex is, well, simple. Just put the frequency into both the transmit and receive sides of the programming software, or put the frequency directly into the radio with no offset frequency or repeater function activated. Yes, it's that simple… dial it in and you can talk on it.

Other 'Interesting' Local Frequencies to Monitor

You can use resources such as www.radioreference.com, www.scannerstuff.com, www.mygmrs.com, and www.interceptradio.com to get lists of local frequencies used variously by public safety, local, state and federal government, and all types of businesses from the local fast-food joint to mall security companies and just about every other type of radio user imaginable.

AUDIO AND VISUAL SIGNALING

Audio Signaling

When cell and radio communications have failed, or when not available, audio signaling can be accomplished with a whistle, canned air horn, car horn, or even gunshots, but the standard for audio signaling is the whistle.

A whistle intended for emergency signaling must be two things: loud, and resistant to the elements.

Whistles are available in a number of manufacturing materials from titanium to plastic. Get one which will not rust, will not easily break in the pack or pocket, and one that will sound in any weather regardless of the temperature.

The "code" to remember for audio signaling is "three." Three equal blasts of a horn or whistle is internationally recognized as a signal for "help." Three equally spaced gunshots serve the same purpose.

Also, with a whistle or a horn, the internationally recognized SOS signal can be used. Three short (one second) blasts followed by three long (three second) blasts, followed by three more short blasts spells out SOS in Morse Code: . . . - - - . . .

There is no reason not to have an emergency whistle in your pack when venturing into the outdoors. They are light, inexpensive, and might save your life.

Visual Signals

The type of visual signal depends on the environment, but the point is to make your presence and location known to rescuers, to get their attention.

The most widely carried visual signaling device on land is the signaling mirror and the flashlight. Obviously one can be used in the daytime and the other at night, but the principle is the same as with audio signaling: three flashes, or the SOS signal.

Some LED flashlights come with the SOS feature built-in, some have a momentary switch, or a steady light can be blocked with the hand or a piece of solid material.

The signaling mirror is available as a standard mirror made of a non-breakable material such as polished stainless steel, or with a hole used as an aiming devise.

The easiest way to aim a signaling mirror is to hold the mirror in one hand near the eye. With the other arm extended, make a V with two fingers and place the target in the middle of the V. Angle the mirror to position the light reflected from the sun on both fingers. When the light is reflected on both fingers and the target is in the V, the reflected light can be seen by the target. Three flashes in rapid or equal succession represents the international distress signal.

It is noteworthy that if you are trying to signal an airplane, it is best to signal when the plane is coming toward you or up to ninety degrees to the airplane. Also, it is easier to get the attention of small planes than an airliner flying at thirty thousand feet. The small plane may also divert to further investigate the flashes, where an airliner will not.

Fire and Smoke

Fire and smoke can be used for signaling, but care must be exercised so as not to ignite vegetation which may lead to a forest fire and place you in even greater peril. Use a large, flat, clear area if possible.

During darkness, build three fires in a triangle and keep them burning. (There's that three again). If you are on the side of a mountain, try to place the fires on the side facing the most civilization, but the fires can be seen from passing aircraft either way.

During daylight, build a fire to generate smoke. Three columns if the area is large enough, but one will suffice if not. The idea is to generate smoke that contrasts to the sky. On a cloudy day white smoke works best, where against a light blue sky dark smoke may work better. White smoke can be generated by smothering the fire with green leaves, green pine, or even putting water on the fire. Dark smoke can be generated using rubber or oil. Not that I would normally recommend burning rubber or putting oil on a fire, but when life is on the line, I'd do it and ignore the environmentalists.

Signaling on Snow, Desert, or Beach

As with any type of visual signal, make as obvious a signal as you can create.

Pine boughs work equally well on both sand and snow. Find as large of an open area as possible to place your signal. You want it well visible from the air, and from a distance.

Make a large X, or a large circle, or circle with an X, make arrows pointing to your location, or even spell out SOS.

On sand, you can use logs or rocks to make the same signals.

Whether making signals on sand or in snow, be sure to create as much contrast as possible, making the signal clearly visible from the air.

At night, fires may be used for signaling if the snow is cleared, or fires placed away from the water's edge on the beach.

PREPPER AND NEIGHBORHOOD COMMUNICATIONS

The word "prepper" brings to mind the eccentric old geezer who has a stockpile of weapons and ammo sufficient to equip a squad of Marines, and is ready to live underground in a bunker, or location in the woods, until all the zombies are exterminated, the lights come back on, and the earth is repopulated.

Though there may be a few of those out there, that's not what a "prepper" really is. A "prepper" is one who prepares. First, for the most likely events which cause the disruption of normal life. It could be weather-related events, job loss, or the electricity being off for a week or longer. We have experienced all three.

In North Central and Central Alabama the most likely event we will encounter is damaging weather events. Alabama actually has more tornadoes per year that Oklahoma's "Tornado Alley." For that reason, we try to be prepared to be self sustaining for three to four weeks at all times. That means four weeks of food, water, a way to cook as well as a way to stay warm, and yes, to be able to protect ourselves if the need arises.

There are many who want to be prepared to communicate during and after a disaster or calamity, whether it be with family, neighbors, or even a prepper group.

The radios covered in this book, or similar radios, are ideal for two-way communications on a local level, whether it is through GMRS/FRS, or other pre-agreed-upon frequencies being used. In fact, at the time of this writing, the Beofeng® handheld dual-band radio is the best selling radio in the prepper community, and you can't beat the price.

In Conclusion

Utilize the methods covered in the section on radios. Program them and practice. Study and take the amateur radio test. It will open a new world and be a great hobby. Reminder: Do not transmit on the HAM radio frequencies without a license, unless it is a true emergency.

Decide if there is equipment you may need to add to your pack, vehicle, or boat when you go into the outdoors. Practice the techniques discussed in this book. Make them into family games. Make them fun.

Be safe. Be prepared. Disasters happen sometimes. Be ready to communicate and get help, if you are injured, lost, stranded, or trapped.

##########

Thank you for reading our book. Please take a moment to leave a review. These really help increase the availability of the book.

Look for our next book, "The Practical Prepper" coming in the fall of 2019.

Contact us at mark@marklawley.us